Six Keys to Breakthrough in Healing

six keys to
BREAKTHROUGH
in healing

by Bill Prankard

Guardian
B O O K S

Belleville, Ontario, Canada

Six Keys to Breakthrough in Healing

Copyright © 2004, Bill Prankard

First printing August 2004
Second printing December 2004

Library and Archives Canada Cataloguing in Publication

Prankard, Bill, 1945-
   Six keys to breakthrough in healing / Bill Prankard.

Includes bibliographical references.
ISBN 1-55306-868-8

   1. Prankard, Bill, 1945- 2. Spiritual healing. 3. Healing--
Religious aspects--Christianity. I. Title.

BT732.5.P734 2004   234'.131   C2004-905011-7

For more information, please contact:

Bill Prankard
Bill Prankard Evangelistic Association,
Box 7007, Station V, Ottawa, ON K1L 8E2
www.bpea.com

Guardian Books is an imprint of *Essence Publishing,* a Christian Book Publisher dedicated to furthering the work of Christ through the written word. For more information, contact: 20 Hanna Court, Belleville, Ontario, Canada K8P 5J2. Phone: 1-800-238-6376 • Fax: (613) 962-3055.
publishing@essencegroup.com • www.essencegroup.com

Chapter One

Paid in Full

I remember ministering to a young woman several years ago. She had been in ministry for quite some time, as had I, but recently found herself in the hospital. She had developed a rather serious chronic condition that the doctors couldn't figure out how to treat or cure. I began to pray and encourage her with the Word of God by talking about the healing scriptures and recounting the promises of God. She put her hand up and said "I know all that, I've been to Bible school, I've been there, I've done that, I've declared it, I've preached it, but it's just not working!" She had come to a point of frustration in her life where she felt she wasn't seeing breakthrough and didn't want to be told what she had already heard.

There are many today who know all the scriptures, own all the tapes, have heard all the teachings on healing, but still have not seen breakthrough—either in their own lives, or in the lives of those whom they're believing for. Because they know that God is faithful and His Word is true, they say, "We must be doing something wrong."

Why is it that we're not seeing the kind of break-throughs we should? First John 5:14 tells us, *"Now this is the confidence that we have in Him, that if we ask anything according to His will, He hears us."*

Every prayer that a believer prays is actually heard in heaven! So, when you say, "My prayers just bounce off the ceiling," or, as a good friend once told me, *"You* pray for me—'cause God's not listening to *me!"* that just isn't the case. God does hear you, even when it seems that He doesn't.

Perhaps you are one of the many who have said in response to a prophetic word or promise, "I've got lots of these; my shelves are full. I don't want another one. I just want to see it happen." I've got great news for you! We are living in the day of the fulfillment of prophecy when every-thing is speeding up and we are seeing all these things come to pass. *"For all the promises of God in Him are Yes, and in Him Amen...."*[1] Simply stated, God does hear us.

One of the interesting truths I've discovered over the years is this: the time that I feel most ineffective is often the time that I am most effective. There are times when I am ministering and feel as if my words are getting about as far as the edge of the platform and then dropping to the floor. The people are just sitting there, looking at me, and every-thing in me says, "Why don't we just go for lunch or some-thing!" It appears as if they don't like me, they don't agree with the teaching, and, honestly, I feel nothing. Afterwards, people will approach me and say, "Wow, you must read my mail!" or "That was the most amazing meeting I've ever been in!" At that moment it becomes crystal clear who was trying to convince me to stop—and it's certainly not God!

I've been in situations where I've been speaking to someone, trying to get a point across and his answer has been, "I hear you, Bill." People can hear us, but if that's as far as it goes, what's the point? If God *just* hears—if He's just collecting prayers in heaven—what good does that do us?

God not only hears our prayers, but He does promise to answer. Matthew 21:22 says, *"And whatever things you ask in prayer, believing, you will receive."*

You've got to know this: God hears you, and God answers. That sounds pretty basic, but it's amazing how many people in the Church haven't really understood it. To say things like, "My prayers are bouncing off of the ceiling," or "God's not listening," indicates the person really doesn't believe this, or hasn't really got it in his spirit.

I can't emphasize this point enough! If you're praying for someone, you have to first know that God's listening and that God answers. The Bible says, *"Whatever things you ask in prayer, believing...."* So that's the whole thing— you have to come to the point where you just expect that we serve a God who loves to answer prayer.

A critical principle regarding healing is this: you've got to know that it's paid for. I am fairly certain that you would never go to the grocery store, get all of your groceries, pay your money, have the clerk bag them up, and then only take half of what you've paid for, leaving the rest on the counter. The price of groceries being what they are, I don't know anybody who would do that.

The price paid for healing is so absolutely expensive. What Mel Gibson showed in his movie, *The Passion of the Christ*, (which was widely criticized for its graphic violence), had to be downplayed. The torture, beatings, and crucifixion were far more brutal than he portrayed in the movie. That was the price paid for healing. If Jesus paid that high a price, the very least we can do is take what's been paid for.

Even before the death of Christ, Isaiah prophetically said *"...and by His stripes we are healed."*[2] Then, on the cross, Jesus mustered every ounce of strength left in Him and triumphantly declared, *"It is finished!,"*[3] so Peter could refer to the words of Isaiah and declare it as a finished work, saying, *"...by whose stripes you were healed."*[4]

Healing was paid for at Calvary. It's not a matter of people coming to God saying, "Lord if it's Your will, please heal me." If He's already paid for it, then, of course, it's His will! Jesus has already gone through the pain and agony and suffering, paying the price so that every one of us might receive what He's paid for.

First Corinthians 6:20 says, *"You were bought at a price...."* Most people stop reading there and assume it means a spiritual purchase. However, if you continue reading the verse, you'll discover it says, *"You were bought at a price;, **therefore** glorify God in your **body** and in your spirit, which are God's"* (emphasis mine). The Bible tells us that God receives glory when you are well—physically, spiritually, emotionally. Jesus wants you to be whole. What a price He paid for it!

Why is it that God chooses to heal both believers and non-believers alike? Christians see non-believers often healed before them and don't understand it. The fact is He heals non-believers out of His compassion and mercy. We also see it as a way of Jesus drawing them to Himself.

At times, believers receive healing because of God's mercy. If we are going to see consistent results, however, we need something we can solidly stand upon, knowing that we're grounded on truth. We must depend on more than a hit-and-miss approach, such as, "If God likes me maybe He'll heal me today," or, "If God is pleased with me today, maybe He'll heal me." No, as believers, we must know we have a covenant promise, according to the Word of God, and have every right to ask for healing.

The purpose behind writing this book is my desire to raise up an army of healing evangelists. I believe that you will become so obsessed with this that you will go out and heal the sick. Your hands, anointed by the power of God, are about to do severe damage to the kingdom of darkness!

In the next seven chapters, we will be discussing keys to breakthrough in healing. If you, or the people you are praying for, aren't getting healed, we suggest that you very tactfully go through these six keys and ask them, "Could it be...?"

---

[1] 2 Corinthians 1:20.

[2] Isaiah 53:5.

[3] John 19:30.

[4] 1 Peter 2:24.

Chapter Two

Unconfessed Sin

"Consider now: Who, being innocent, has ever perished? Where were the upright ever destroyed? As I have observed, those who plow evil and those who sow trouble reap it" (Job 4:7,8 NIV).

"There is sin in your life, and that is why you are sick!" That, in essence, is what Job's three friends told him after he lost his family, possessions, and his very health. Job, knowing that he was pure before God, could have reacted violently towards his "encouragers," but instead chose to, once again, search his heart.

I am not telling you that you are sick because you have sin in your life, nor am I telling you that the person you are praying for has sin in his life. John 3:17 reads, *"For God did not send His Son into the world to condemn the world, but that the world through Him might be saved."* Jesus is not in the condemnation business, nor should we be.

This is not a matter of condemnation, but of making

sure your heart is in the place it should be. You need to
ensure that there's nothing blocking your relationship with
God so that when you come to Him, as your Father, you're
coming with a pure heart and not trying to hide anything
from Him. He knows our hearts and wants us to approach
Him with honesty. When we do that, we can be absolutely
assured that He will accept us with open arms. Because
Father God loves us that much, we never have to fear
coming to Him in whatever state we're in, whether we feel
we're in good standing with Him, or whether we are so far
gone that we just think that nobody could ever receive us.

God wants to be in relationship with us—that was the
reason we were created in the first place. In Genesis,
before sin came between God and man, we see God literally walking and talking with Adam and Eve, spending
time and building relationships with them. Now, just as it
was then, when there are things in our lives that block our
relationships with God, it grieves Him. Not because He
wants to condemn us, but because our relationships with
him are hindered.

He asks us to come to Him with honesty, just as Job did.
In Psalms, David prayed, *"Search me, O God, and know
my heart; try me, and know my anxieties: And see if there
is any wicked way in me...."*[1]

David had to come to God confessing some pretty horrendous sins and yet found a loving Father ready to receive
him. Psalm 32:3, 4 says,

> *When I refused to confess my sin, I was weak and
> miserable, and I groaned all day long. Day and
> night your hand of discipline was heavy on me. My
> strength evaporated like water in the summer heat.
> Finally, I confessed all my sins to you and stopped*

trying to hide them. I said to myself, "I will confess my rebellion to the Lord (NLT).

The result of David's confession of sin is recorded in the remainder of Psalm 32 and continues through several chapters. David found victory, relationship, and amazing joy, because he came to God in repentance. You and I can have that same wonderful, open relationship with God too!

Please understand, God heals people who have sin in their lives. God heals non-believers. I've seen people come to our healing revival meetings over the years, who have stood up, challenged everything I've said, and gone so far as to commit what I would consider to be blasphemy, yet God often heals them. In such instances, God is not condoning that person's actions, but rather saying, "I love you!" Often, at the end of a service, the people giving their lives to Christ are the very same unbelieving people He healed. They've felt God's love.

As a Christian seeking to walk consistently in healing and health, or if you want more than hit-and-miss results when you minister healing, this is an important key: *"Confess your sins… that you may be healed."*[2]

In the previous chapter, I wrote that God hears us, but Isaiah qualifies that statement by saying, sin separates us from God.

"Behold the Lord's hand is not shortened, that it cannot save; nor His ear heavy, that it cannot hear. But your iniquities have separated you from your God and your sins have hidden His face from you, so that He will not hear."[3]

He hears us when we come to Him with an open heart, without trying to hide anything from Him. If we come to

God in honesty, He will hear, but if we try to keep our sins hidden, hoping He will somehow overlook them, the Bible tells us that He will not hear. We cannot expect that God is consistently going to bring healing into our lives if we haven't come to a place of complete honesty and repentance before Him.

Some time ago, while we were traveling, I saw a license plate that read, "O WELL." I thought, "Isn't that a typical attitude of some Christians?" There have been a lot of people in the Church that have said, "I know I should do this," or " I know I shouldn't be into this, but 'O WELL,'" and then they wonder why they are not seeing the blessings of God. Thank God the wind of holiness is blowing! The closer you get to wonderful Jesus and the closer and more intimate you become with the Holy Spirit, the more He reveals to you.

You or I might think we're doing fine, until we have an experience in which you see His glory. Peter, after seeing the glory of God revealed in Jesus, said, *Depart from me, for I am a sinful man, O Lord!*[4]

A dimly-lit room may appear to be clean, but when a bright light is brought into that same room, a covering of dust on the tables, or dirt in the corners may be noticed. That was Peter's experience. The light of God's glory allowed him to see the sin in his life that he otherwise would not have seen.

Don't let anything hinder. There are so many in the Body of Christ who have harboured sin in their hearts and then wonder why they are sick, why they aren't getting healed.

When you're ministering to someone and the person is just not breaking through, please don't look at him and say, "You must be a filthy sinner, and you're on your way to hell!" or "You must have sin in your heart." People get offended by that! They put walls up. Instead, you could very nicely say, "Why don't you start by asking the Lord if there is anything hindering breakthrough in your life? Maybe you're not even conscious of it, but would you ask the Holy Spirit to reveal it to you?"

That's the first step. Refusing to deal with hidden sin will block the blessing of God. When you're ministering to people and they're not breaking through (and it's wonderful when they do), take them through this first step.

If they've searched their hearts and know things are right between them and the Lord, take them to the next step.

---

1 Psalm 139:23–24.

2 James 5:16, NIV.

3 Isaiah 59:1–2.

4 Luke 5:8.

Chapter Three

Honour

"Honor your father and your mother, that your days may be long upon the land which the Lord your God is giving you" (Exodus 20:12).

I was ministering in Edmonton, Alberta, about ten years ago, talking about God's love and loving others. At the end of the service, I felt led to have the worship team sing that very simple, little-children's song, "Jesus Loves Me." It was a very sweet time in God's presence, and people were genuinely touched by the simplicity of God's love. Towards the end of that altar time, a lady approached me. She was visibly upset.

I was brought up in a relatively functional family, having parents that loved, cared, and protected me. They brought me up in a godly home, and so it's hard to comprehend when I'm confronted with stories like the one this lady told me.

"Are you telling me that I have to love and forgive my father?" she began, tears in her eyes. I knew there was more to the question, so I just waited for her to continue. "Every night since I turned seven, my father would come into my room and sexually abuse me."

"O God," I thought, "I can't imagine how awful that would be—I can't imagine the hurt!"

She went on, "I hurt so badly, and I felt so dirty. The abuse continued for years, night after night. After he'd leave, I'd go into my closet and close the door. I had a big blanket in there that I'd pull over my head and curl up with on the floor, hoping he wouldn't come back and find me. I would sing 'Jesus loves me, this I know, for the Bible tells me so....'" She stopped, looked directly into my eyes and said, "You're telling me, I have to forgive him—you're telling me, I have to honour him?"

This young lady was not living a full, healthy life. And make no mistake, sadly, her story is by no means an isolated case. For obvious reasons, people like her have great difficulty giving honour to their parents. I honestly can't even imagine pain like she had experienced. But sooner or later, she would have to come to grips with this scriptural key to healing.

What does honouring your parents have to do with healing? According to the scriptures, if you want to be free from sickness, disease, and pain, you must find a way to honour your parents.

In reality, it has very little to do with what your father and mother did or didn't do, but rather, about your living a long, full, and healthy life. In many cases, such as the one I described, there are parents who absolutely do not deserve any kind of honour. I understand that; but for you not to do what the Bible teaches allows them to continue to hurt you. That's the bottom line. According to Exodus, a lot of people aren't living a long, full, healthy life, and the issue of honour is at the heart of it.

There is no question that abusive, sadistic parents must be held accountable for their actions. The victim, however, must deal with the emotional and physical scars that result from the abuse. But once it is dealt with, the victim must move forward.

No matter what horrendous treatment you may have suffered in the past, there are some things about your parents that you can acknowledge and honour. Even if your parents are no longer living, you can still honour their memory. If the only good thing you can think of to say is that they brought you into the world, then say that! You can't change your past, but you do determine your destiny! If that is honestly the only good thing you've got, simply say, "Thank You God that there were two people that brought me into this world and now I can be used by You!"

There's a story that's told of a man who was walking along the street one day, when a seagull flew overhead and did what seagulls sometimes do—dropped something—and that's not a very nice thing. (Trust me on this—I know—but that's another story.) The mess landed on the man's head. Naturally he was very upset about what the seagull did to him.

He arrived at his home in this condition and tried to put his arm around his wife to hug and kiss her. His wife pulled away from him, not allowing him to get close because of all the "seagull stuff" on him. This upset the man even more. "It's not my fault!" the man said. "The seagull did this to me."

A little while later, his children came into the room. The man tried to greet them with a hug and kiss, but they too pushed away from him. Again he protested, "I can't help it.

The seagull did this to me." He became increasingly angry at the seagull.

The next day he went into the store where he worked and stood behind the counter as he always had done. Customers quickly became repulsed at the sight and smell of the man and left the store. In turn, the man's boss became angry at him for driving the customers away and fired him. The man then became even more upset as he cried, "It's not my fault, the seagull did this to me!"

He continued to live with the mess on his head, blaming the seagull for his misfortunes, until finally he not only lost his job, but his wife, family and friends. He came to a point where he was penniless and living under a bridge in a cardboard box. Every day he'd crawl out from under the bridge, shake his fist at the sky and shout, "This is what the seagull did to me!" And every day he would wait for the seagull to return and correct what had gone so terribly wrong.

Of course, it's a very unlikely story, but isn't that how it is with a lot of people? They stay in a victim mentality, constantly blaming the person who wronged them. Certainly, that person is accountable to God and owes a great debt for the wrongs committed. The fact is, however, if you continue to stay in that place of victimization—you will never get beyond that. You will continue to live in a state of hate, unforgiveness, and bitterness until you can finally say, "I acknowledge what happened to me, but God, help me reach out beyond these circumstances that are holding me prisoner and help me to get on with my life."

Yes, deal with the emotional pain. Yes, deal with the consequences of whatever injustice you suffered, but then get up, move on, and let God use you. It is vital that you get beyond the victimization point to a place where you are not only a survivor, not only an overcomer, but someone who is, as the Bible says, *"more than conquerors"*[1]!

Gwen has worn eyeglasses for nearsightedness from the age of twelve. In addition, she has been on medication since 1993 to correct an under-active thyroid condition. Initially, she diligently pursued healing for these conditions, but since both were easily corrected medically and just a minor inconvenience, over time, she rarely thought to keep believing for healing.

About five years ago, while spending a couple of rare days at a cottage with our daughter Margie and her family, Gwen woke up early to read and pray alone by the lake. Suddenly a long forgotten memory came to her.

Her mother had died when she was only thirteen, leaving her to be raised by her father, who was in his sixties at the time. He rarely showed any kind of emotion with his children. In addition, he had been raised as a homesteader on the Canadian prairies, living through the great depression in severe poverty. As a result, he held on to every penny he earned with a tight fist. Gwen and her older sister, along with having to take care of all the household chores and going to school, worked part-time jobs from the time they were preteens. The income they earned was their only source for whatever clothes, school supplies, and personal essentials they needed. As a youngster, she couldn't understand that the struggles of her father's early life made him so frugal. She simply thought he was stingy.

Her father passed away when Gwen was in her late twenties. Although she shed a few tears, she often wondered why she hadn't felt the deep grief and sense of loss she had experienced when her mother died. The thought nagged at her occasionally, but she never connected it to an issue of the heart. Now, as she sat by the lake praying, the memory of her father came flooding over her. She suddenly realized she had been holding resentment in her heart toward him all these years! The tears came streaming down her face as she repented and allowed Jesus to release the pain.

Since that lakeside experience, there have been some interesting developments concerning Gwen's health. She began to notice that it bothered her to wear her glasses for certain activities, such as watching television. After testing her eyes, the puzzled optometrist said, "Your prescription is too strong. Normally eyes deteriorate as they get older, but yours have really improved!" Shortly after this good news, she had blood tests taken to check her thyroid levels. Originally, the doctor had told Gwen the thyroid would continue to deteriorate, until she would be totally dependant on medication for its function. The doctor was amazed that it was now functioning better than before! That prescription was scaled down as well!

It amazes me how some people talk about their parents. Maybe they're joking, or being sarcastic, but it's amazing how they bring dishonour to their mother or father. If you haven't got anything good to say, it's best not to say anything at all.

I grew up, as I said, in a great family, but wasn't especially close to my dad. I sometimes joke that my family resembled the one depicted on the television show, "Everybody Loves Raymond." Just like Raymond, my mother loved me very much. After she passed away though, I realized, that although my dad and I cared very much for each other, we just didn't have the same sense of closeness as Mom and I. Mom had done all the talking on the phone and wrote all the letters on behalf of Dad and her. Then, all of a sudden, she was gone. I made a decision that, because I really didn't know my dad like I wanted to know him, I would make a concerted effort to build a relationship with this man.

No matter where I was in Canada during the last several years of my dad's life, I did my best to get back to Brampton, where he lived, once a week for breakfast. I would pick him up at 7:00 a.m., and although he'd have already eaten breakfast two hours earlier, we'd go out and have another. We spent the time just sitting and talking, and I'd say, "Tell me about this.... Tell me the stories about that...." The result was an amazing relationship with my dad.

Whatever your relationship is with your parents, it is not too late to honour them. Even if your mother or father is gone, you can still honour them. That may sound spooky, I know, but just begin simply by sharing the good memories you have.

I think it would be appropriate, right now, to allow the Holy Spirit to bring at least one positive thing into your heart and mind about your mother and your father. Many times we focus on the negative—but think of one positive thing. If you honestly can't recall at least one positive memory, remind yourself that they brought you into the world. That truly is a good thing! The world is a better place because you're here. Just go ahead and thank God for your mother and father. Some of you will find that very difficult, but remember, it's not about them—it's about you being healed and getting on the road to, what Exodus talks about, having "a long, full life." A *long* life means you've faced and conquered challenges along the way. A *full* life means you're enjoying good health, happiness, and abundance—and it comes when you honour your father and mother.

The Bible doesn't stop with parents when it speaks of relationships. Read 1 Peter 3:7, *"Husbands, likewise, dwell with them with understanding, giving honor to the wife, as to the weaker vessel, and as being heirs together of the grace of life, that your prayers may not be hindered."*

So often in this passage and similar ones, we get stuck on *"husbands, honor your wives,"* or *"wives, submit to your husbands,"* but if we read the end of verse seven, it says, *"...that your prayers may not be hindered."* Think about it. If you don't honour your partner, it's going to hurt you; your prayers will be hindered!

We try to separate this by reasoning, "My prayer life is between me and God. It has nothing to do with others."

We've been with some Christian couples who, in some ways, are very entertaining to watch, as they take verbal "digs" at one another. Yet, it's so sad. The verbal abuse that they call "good-natured" is at times overwhelming when you think, "I can't imagine what they're like in private, if they are so unkind to each other in public!" It never ceases to amaze me that a man could so easily degrade his wife, or a wife humiliate her husband, especially in light of the verse we've just read in 1 Peter 3! It is all about their prayers being answered.

Husbands, honour your wives. You need to work at it. All of us in marriage have had high times and low times, good times and bad times. This summer my wife, Gwen, and I celebrate forty years of wedded bliss. For the past several years we have been virtually inseparable, travelling and ministering together in almost every circumstance. That, however, wasn't always the case. When our children were younger, Gwen stayed at home with them much of the time, as I ministered in various parts of the country. She divided her time between her care for the family at home and the occasional brief ministry assignment with me, ensuring our children were in the care of others as little as possible. The nature of my calling as an evangelist meant I had to be away from home several days each week. It was on our twenty-fifth anniversary that someone asked the secret of our marital success. Gwen jokingly responded that it had been seven of the happiest years of her life, (suggesting that, when you add up the days we'd actually been together over the twenty-five years, they amounted to about seven years)!

After my dramatic encounter with the Holy Spirit at a Kathryn Kuhlman service in 1972, our lives changed drastically, launching us into national healing evangelism. We were not prepared for what we'd been thrust into, and both our personal lives and ministry seemed to be thrown into a state of chaos. We didn't know anything about spiritual warfare—we didn't expect Christians to be attacking and threatening to destroy us—it was quite an amazing time. In the midst of it, our marriage really went through some tough times, as I struggled to come to terms with the sudden "success," Gwen tried to cope with a sense of insignificance, left behind with all the family and household responsibilities. As the walls of isolation and resentment grew between us, we came to a point, back in the early 1970s when we felt our marriage was doomed for failure and actually briefly considered separating.

The one thing we had been praying for, during all of our years of ministry together, happened. We'd prayed fervently and consistently for revival, both in us and in the congregations we were pastoring. We had prayer meetings every week seeking God, praying for a supernatural outpouring of the Holy Spirit. Suddenly He answered our prayers! Yet we were totally unprepared for the consequences.

We were pastoring a little country church with a congregation of fifty or sixty people when overnight, as miraculous healings began taking place, we couldn't accommodate the crowds that came. People often sat outside the church on the lawn, or stood on the sidewalks, straining to hear or see what was taking place inside. We had to put sound equipment outside, so the huge crowds of people could at least hear what was going on inside! People were being healed and saved, both inside and outside the church. We eventually moved to a larger auditorium where hundreds of people—more than the total population of the little village—would come every week to the healing meetings. It really was an amazing revival that happened in the Ottawa Valley.

The downside was that all of this happened so suddenly that we weren't prepared for the dramatic changes that would affect both the congregation and us as a couple. I began to receive invitations to minister in large churches across the nation. I flew all over the country and stayed in the nicest hotels. People thronged to the meetings and constantly boosted my ego, telling me how wonderful I was. Many weeks I'd be gone from home Monday to Saturday, returning home for the Sunday services, then flying off again the following Monday.

Meanwhile, Gwen had the sole care of our four little children (one in kindergarten and three preschoolers), the household, and whatever church responsibilities arose in my absence. The responsibility resting on her shoulders quickly turned to resentment. Even though she had prayed for revival just as sincerely as I had, she wasn't ready for the emotional turmoil that resulted. She struggled with a terrible sense of guilt, torn apart by the responsibilities of home and church and her sense of insignificance in the new ministry focus I was enjoying.

My experience was completely the opposite! I'd often return home following a successful crusade, where multitudes of people had been saved, healed, and delivered, expecting Gwen to be excited and enthused about "my" success. More likely, she'd ask me to take Margie to school, or say, "It's time to take out the trash."

With my newly-inflated ego, I was tempted to ask, "Don't you realize who I am?" Ordinary chores like these were suddenly "beneath" me. The problem was, Gwen did know who I was—and she didn't like what she saw! She has since teased me that one day she's going to write a book entitled, *Great Men of God Have to Put Out the Garbage Too!*

We both knew something had to change. I was obsessed with reaching the whole world for Christ, at the expense of everyone and everything else, and Gwen was becoming increasingly resentful and withdrawn. I prayed privately, "Lord, change Gwen," not knowing she was praying, "Lord, change Bill." We were self-destructing.

If you asked us then what had to change, I would have said, "Gwen has to change this, has to stop doing that; Gwen has to do such and such...." And Gwen most definitely would have said, "Bill has to stop doing this; Bill has to change that; Bill has to do such and such...."

Before our situation became completely out of control, I had a real experience with God. It was just after a meeting where hundreds of people had been healed and saved. I went back to the hotel room and sat in the dark, all alone.

Jesus visited me that night and showed me that, in striving for "success," I was losing what was most precious to me, my family. That night I gave my pride, my wife and my children over to Him. I returned home a changed man.

I began to honour Gwen. Our prayers started being answered in a totally different way. As she saw the change in me, the walls between us began to crumble. God showed both of us exactly what we needed to change and exactly how to do it. I adjusted my travelling schedule so that I was seldom away more than three or four days at a time. Gwen made arrangements to accompany me on occasional ministry trips. He dealt with us about our attitudes and gave us a promise that we wouldn't lose our marriage, our kids, or the wonderful ministry he'd entrusted to us, if we obeyed Him and did it His way.

You can hear the Word, you can know the scriptures, but if you're going to have a successful healing ministry, you have to act on the keys He's given you, including honouring one another. You must do more than just hear. James said it best, *"But be **doers** of the **word**, and not hearers only, deceiving yourselves."*[2]

God wants you to keep going until Jesus returns! He doesn't want your effectiveness to be a "flash-in-the-pan," experiencing short-lived results, losing your family, home, and everything else in the process. No! God wants your ministry, both public and private, to flourish and succeed. Begin honouring each other and your prayers will not be hindered.

---

[1] Romans 8:37.

[2] James 1:22, emphasis mine.

Chapter Four

If You Can't Say Anything Nice...

"Who is the man who desires life, and loves many days, that he may see good? Keep your tongue from evil, and your lips from speaking deceit. Depart from evil and do good; seek peace and pursue it" (Psalm 34:12–14).

I'm not sure when or how it happened, but, several years ago, God gave us an appreciation for the diversity of ministries within the Body of Christ. We have an awesome respect for all of those ministering and serving Him even though their ministries may all differ drastically.

A few years ago, a dear friend, Tommy Reid, who pastors a great church in Buffalo, New York, invited me to go with him to Boston for lunch with Robert Schuller. I readily accepted because Dr. Schuller is a man I hold in high esteem. My son-in-law, Mike, accompanied me to share the driving responsibilities.

A few years prior, I went through a depression. It was a

very difficult time for me, particularly since I didn't believe in being depressed! For weeks, I tried to "snap out of it," with no success, but every Sunday morning, Robert Schuller would come on TV and announce, "This is the day the Lord has made...."[1] His message of positive faith and possibility thinking would inject me with such hope—it was like taking medicine every Sunday morning.

What an honour it was to sit across the table from him and tell him how God had used him to spark something fresh in my life and bring healing!

That same evening, we drove to New York City to visit David Wilkerson. Years before, I'd ministered at a conference where David was speaking, and he'd invited Gwen and me to spend a week at his Texas ranch and ministry headquarters. Several years later, as he returned to New York to begin Time Square Church, he gave an open invitation for us to visit him there as well. Mike and I had a late dinner with him, talking about the goodness of God and sharing together. It was amazing to receive such insight and encouragement from two highly respected men with very diverse ministry perspectives.

I called Gwen from my hotel room later that night and told her, "I had lunch with Robert Schuller and dinner with David Wilkerson. I feel pretty balanced today!"

Both men, Robert Schuller and David Wilkerson, are wonderful men of God, each with a specific message, a unique voice, but at vastly different ends of the spectrum. Many prominent ministries today have a different emphasis, but when you combine what each is saying with the others and listen to the overall message, you begin to get a fully-orbed understanding of what God is saying to the Church today.

I am so grateful for every ministry that has something to say to the Body of Christ today. I'm thankful that, because of them, we are where we are today. Some critics accuse particular ministries' teaching as "extreme," but— whether it's John & Carol Arnott, who have so eloquently introduced people to the Father's heart, ministries like Kenneth Copeland, or the Hagens, who are so strong in the area of faith and standing on the Word of God, or a man like David Wilkerson, who has such a strong prophetic edge and message of repentance—each has an important word for the Church today. As we take all of these truths together and put them into practice in our lives, we're going to be truly balanced.

Psalms 34:12 asks who wants a good, healthy life? I don't know anyone who would answer, "not me!"

The psalmist answers his own question and continues,

Keep your tongue from evil, and your lips from speaking deceit [or guile]. Depart from evil do good; seek peace and pursue it. The eyes of the Lord are on the righteous and His ears are open to their cry.[2]

Be careful how you talk about other people. The Bible very plainly tells us, if we want a long and healthy life, we need to watch what we say. Some Christians seem to be very good at ripping apart ministers and ministries. It has been said that the Church is the only army that shoots its wounded. Perhaps another accurate statement would be, "The Church is the only army that takes potshots at its generals!"

"It would be easy, for example, if you were healed at a Benny Hinn crusade, to disregard any other ministries. It's only natural that, because you were touched in one of his meetings, you continue to watch his telecast, or support his ministry financially. The danger comes, however, when you begin to criticize other ministries and have no appreciation for anyone that's doing or saying anything different.

There are, of course, ministries in the body that seem to overemphasize a particular truth. In most instances, I believe, it is because there has been a lack in the body. Just as a doctor would sometimes prescribe a heavy dose of medication to make up for missed treatments, so it is in the Church. Thank God for any ministry that is strong in the area of faith, discipleship, healing, or repentance, but make sure that you feed on "the whole counsel of God." If you can also appreciate other ministries that God has placed in the body, you will get a balanced diet.

From time to time, someone will approach me and say something negative about another ministry. My response to them is always, "When you're reaching as many people for Jesus as that ministry is, then maybe we can talk...."

Gwen makes this analogy: if you are standing out in the rain, but have an umbrella over your head, you are protected from the downpour. The moment you move out from under the umbrella, you are going to get wet. In the same way, God has provided us with an "umbrella of protection" from sickness and disease. We stay protected from these attacks when we live within the principles and conditions He has set out. Guarding our tongue is one of them. When we violate these conditions, we, in effect, walk out from under God's umbrella, allowing ourselves to be susceptible to everything the enemy might try to pour on us.

It's a sad fact that Christians can do a great deal of damage to each other. We need to guard our tongues. We need to watch what we say. It used to be that when another Christian brother or sister was struggling, people would go to prayer. They would fight for that person or ministry until they broke through and saw restoration and healing. Sadly, that doesn't happen as often as it should. Instead, people petition, gossip, and criticize, often under the guise of a "prayer request."

Make up your mind today to *"keep your tongue from evil, and your lips from speaking deceit."*[3] It is another key to breakthrough in healing!

----

[1] Psalm 118:24.
[2] Psalm 34:12–15.
[3] Psalm 34:13.

Chapter Five

Forgive

"Therefore if you bring your gift to the altar, and there remember that your brother has something against you, leave your gift there before the altar, and go your way. First be reconciled to your brother, and then come and offer your gift" (Matthew 5:23,24).

The Bible repeatedly shows us that answered prayer often hinges on atonement, that is, making wrongs right. Look at the Lord's Prayer in Matthew 6, *"Forgive us our debts, as we forgive our debtors."*[1]

A woman I consider a hero is a young Inuit lady named Susan Aglukark. Susan's mom and dad have pastored churches in the Canadian Arctic for years. We first met them when they were a young couple pastoring in Rankin Inlet about thirty years ago. Susan, at the time, was just a little kid running around with the others in her village. She has since grown up and experienced great success in her career as a singer, earning several Juno awards and numerous top ten hits. Susan's career, however, was really launched through her response to abuse.

A few years ago, I heard statistics that one of every two girls and one of every three boys, in the north of our nation, will be sexually molested before the age of eighteen.[2] These statistics certainly go a long way to explain the suicide epidemic that is sweeping across the Canadian Arctic. In the Inuit culture, even more than in mainstream Canadian culture, very few people discussed abuse until recently. No one was supposed to talk about it. You simply didn't tell.

For several years, Susan kept quiet about the abuse, bottling up her emotions. One day, however, she somehow found out that the man (a relative, but not in her immediate family), who had violated her, was still abusing other young girls in the community.

Against everything her culture had taught her, she went to the police, reported the man, and charges were laid. During the events that followed, she came south and stayed with us in our home for awhile—to get out of the community, because she was not very popular. Even in her home church, people had questioned her, asking, "Why are you doing this?'

Susan, however, not only saw this man go to jail, but has since become a powerful voice to the hurting young people of the north. She dealt with the issue, moved beyond being a victim, forgave the man involved, and is making her life count for good. We commend her for that. Had she decided to stay in a state of unforgiveness, harbouring resentment towards this man, I can guarantee you that Susan would not have the platform she does now.

The point is this: there is life afterwards! Susan made a decision that the blood of Jesus is strong enough, the cross is powerful enough, and that nothing could keep her from realizing God's destiny for her! In one of her songs, "Dreams for You," she sings, "Daddy, I'm singing my dream."

Until we make things right, we cannot rightfully expect God to answer our prayers. Jesus' disciples were astonished to see a fig tree withered at the roots the day after Jesus cursed it. It was an opportune time for Jesus to teach them about faith. He said,

> *"Have faith in God. For assuredly, I say to you, whoever says to this mountain, 'Be removed and be cast into the sea,' and does not doubt in his heart, but believes that those things he says will come to pass, he will have whatever he says. Therefore I say to you, whatever things you ask when you pray, believe that you receive them, and you will have them."*[3]

The key to receiving healing, as outlined in this passage, appears to be pretty simple. Speak to the mountain—sickness, poverty, bondage, etc.—with faith, without doubt, and your prayer is answered! If we keep reading, however, we find that Jesus' teaching didn't end there. He adds a crucial condition:

> *"And whenever you stand praying, if you have anything against anyone, forgive him, that your Father in heaven may also forgive you your trespasses. But if you do not forgive, neither will your Father in heaven forgive your trespasses."*[4]

Yes, this does sound "easier said than done"! Our pride wants to justify our "right" to withhold forgiveness. But Jesus didn't specify under which conditions we should forgive. He simply said, "forgive."

The simplest way I can tell you how to forgive is this: develop your relationship with Jesus. When you are totally committed and consumed with loving Him, there is no room for self-pity, self-righteousness, or pride. This makes it so easy to forgive those that have wronged you.

Once your focus is totally on God, the next step becomes much easier. Put yourself in the place of those you believe have wronged you. How do they see the situation? What pain and difficulties are they facing? Could past hurts and abuses be causing them to act the way they do? As you continue to put yourself in their place, begin to love them and realize they did not set out to intentionally hurt you. They need love, understanding, and healing in their own lives. Once your attitude toward your "offenders" changes, the groundwork is laid for the act of forgiveness.

My parents and other members of my family became Spirit-filled believers shortly after I fully committed my life to Christ and entered the ministry. At the time, my youngest brother was a teenager, and Mom and Dad had some concerns about his walk with the Lord. They enlisted the prayer support of their pastor and hoped he would make a special effort to encourage my brother in his faith.

A short while later, my mother was diagnosed with an incurable kidney disease. Following weeks of treatment in the hospital, she was released to rest at home, but the doctor cautioned her condition would only deteriorate. He advised her to limit her activities to conserve what little strength remained.

Most of the young people, in the church she attended, called her "Mom Prankard," because of her constantly loving, giving ways. She often took in "strays"—young people with few friends, or ability to afford a place of their own. Her sickness changed all that, but she insisted on going to church each week, just to be in the presence of other believers and to feel a part of those she loved. Dad made it a practice to arrive with Mom shortly after the service began, sit in the back row with her, and take her home before dismissal, to avoid the physical weakness that would result if she stayed to greet the many who loved her and wanted to spend time with her.

One Sunday morning, however, Mom wouldn't let Dad take her home early. When the service was dismissed, she made her way up the aisle to where the pastor was standing. The Lord had revealed to her that she had been holding an attitude of unforgiveness in her heart toward him, because he hadn't made as much effort to encourage my straying brother as she would have liked. She had not been consciously aware of any resentment toward him, but now realized she must ask his forgiveness. Without going into any detail, she threw her arms around him and told him she loved him. At that instant, every symptom of weakness and pain left Mom's body! Tests later confirmed that she was totally healed of the deadly kidney condition. What all of the prayers, faith, and declaration of healing had not done, one simple act of forgiveness did in a moment!

Forgiveness is an act of the will. Paul instructed the believers in Corinth not to deal harshly with an individual who had wronged them, but to, instead, extend forgiveness.

You ought rather to forgive and comfort him, lest perhaps such a one be swallowed up with too much sorrow. Therefore I urge you to reaffirm your love to him. For to this end I also wrote, that I might put you to the test, whether you are obedient in all things. Now whom you forgive anything, I also for-

give. For if indeed I have forgiven anything I have forgiven that one for your sakes in the presence of Christ, lest Satan should take advantage of us; for we are not ignorant of his devices.[5]

I am sure some of the Corinthian believers swallowed hard when they read Paul's instructions! Those who had been wronged likely felt their offender deserved to be ostracized and punished. Paul, though, was telling them to demonstrate true forgiveness by acts of kindness!

Forgiveness is not simply an intellectual decision, but a voluntary act of the will. Jesus *chose* to go to the cross to provide forgiveness, healing, and peace of mind, leaving us an example to follow.[6] When we choose to forgive and demonstrate our decision by actions, we follow Christ's example and use an effective key to unlock the benefits of heaven.

---

[1] Matthew 6:12.

[2] Aboriginal Youth Network, on-line posting. <http:www.ayn.ca/health/en/abuse/abuse_child_sexual.asp>

[3] Mark 11:22–24.

[4] Mark 11:25, 26.

[5] 2 Corinthians 2:7–11.

[6] 1 Peter 2:21–23.

Chapter Six

Don't Accept it

"Do you want to be healed?" (John 5:6 ESV).

Another big hindrance to receiving healing, either for yourself, or for someone you're ministering to, is the willingness to simply accept the condition.

I've heard people say things like: "It runs in the family," "At my age, you have to expect this type of thing," "It's going around, so what can you do," or "The doctor says it's chronic, and there's nothing that can be done." Whatever the circumstance of their sickness or disease, they just accept it!

In a previous chapter, I wrote about the thyroid and nearsightedness problems Gwen had experienced and how God began the healing process. What I didn't tell you, and what she only recently realized, was that she had also come to a place where she had accepted those conditions. When the thyroid problem was first diagnosed, she entered every healing service she was in with an expectation of healing. She didn't accept the conditions as "normal" and constantly believed for a miracle. As time wore on, however, and the medication effectively removed all the symptoms of the thyroid condition, she thought about healing less frequently. A little pill first thing in the morning became routine, and, over time, she came to accept the condition as "no big deal." The same was true of her nearsightedness. She would put her glasses on and forget about it. Soon, she was no longer in a place of believing for her healing, but instead had come to unconsciously accept the two conditions as part of her "normal" life.

It was only recently, since the lakeside experience, that she became aware of the enemy's deception. He had lulled her into dependence on prescription lenses and a little pill, instead of the miracle-working power of God! She began to actively pursue her covenant rights, paid for at Calvary. That decision, along with the change of heart regarding her father, began the healing process that she expects will soon be completed.

You can see how easy it is to accept sickness, or disease, and that is why we have to totally change the way we think, act, and talk! Gwen stopped saying "*my* thyroid condition" or "*my* nearsightedness." She refuses to claim ownership of those conditions.

"*The thief does not come except to steal, and to kill, and to destroy. I have come that they may have life, and that they may have it more abundantly.*"[1]

It is clear that sickness comes from the pit of hell, and yet we often seem almost eager to accept it! A medical condition attacking your body is not "*your* cancer, *your* arthritis, or *your* sickness"; it's from the devil, it belongs to the devil, and it's high time you send it back to the devil!

Have you ever had a sliver in your finger? If so, you

know how that tiny piece of wood irritates and aggravates you. It is a foreign substance that does not belong in your finger, so you dig and poke persistently until it is finally removed. Why not take the same attitude toward sickness? Sickness and disease are not "normal." The "thief" is out to steal your health, while Jesus wants you to live life "more abundantly." God designed you to be strong, healthy, and whole. Anything that interferes with God's design should be treated as a "foreign substance" in your body. Become persistent in faith until it is removed!

In a service some time ago, a man came forward with this strange testimony, "I've lost him!" I was puzzled and asked him, "Who have you lost?" "My friend, Arthur! Arthur-itis is gone!" At the time, I, along with everyone else in the place, found it amusing, but when I thought about it later, it really began to bother me. Like many others, the condition in this man's body had become part of his identity; in fact, in his case, he'd made a friend of it! We should not accept, tolerate, live with, get by with, put up with, or endure sickness in our lives, let alone befriend it. Your attitude about sickness, to a large extent, may very well determine whether you're going to be healed, or not—or if you're going to have a successful healing ministry, or not.

I often invite people forward for prayer and ask what it is they're praying for. Some tell me that they've had such-and-such a condition for thirty years, or whatever, so I'll say, "Let's believe God for healing!" Their immediate response is (and I can't believe they come for prayer and still respond this way), "Well, I've had it for thirty years...."

It's almost as if they're saying, "You really don't expect me to get healed, do you?" Following prayer, I ask them to check the condition. Many times I see their reluctance, and, in fact, some have said, "I've been prayed for lots of times, and I didn't get healed." It's like they've come to God saying, "Okay, Lord, give it your best shot... but...." No wonder they don't get healed!

Our whole attitude towards health and healing has got to change! Often we don't really expect to be healed, and, even worse, have come to a place of not only accepting our condition, but embracing it. That includes a lot of people who have a destiny, those that God has called to minister. Because of their physical conditions, they aren't able to do what they've been called to do. Yet, it never seems to occur to them that the enemy is depriving them of God's purpose for their lives.

John 5 relates the story of a sick man lying near the Pool of Bethesda, along with crowds of other sick or disabled people. At various times an angel came and stirred up the water. Miraculously, the first person to step into the pool, while the water was stirred, would be healed. When Jesus saw the man and learned he had been there for thirty-eight years, he asked him a question, *"Do you want to be healed?"*[2]

It was a curious thing to ask.. Of course, the man *wanted* to be healed, didn't he? Why else would he stay year after year near the pool? The man's response is revealing.

"I can't, sir," the sick man said, "for I have no one to help me into the pool when the water is stirred up. While I am trying to get there, someone else always gets in ahead of me."[3]

Here's the point: Jesus didn't ask the man *why* he hadn't been healed before. He asked him if he *wanted* to be healed. This man was not very different than many of us. We look at all the reasons it can't happen, instead of recognizing the Miracle-worker right in front of us!

"Jesus told him, "Stand up, pick up your sleeping mat, and walk!"[4] Remember, this man had been lying there for thirty-eight years! But Jesus was asking him to *do* something, just as he expects us to take the first step toward our miracle! When the man responded, he was instantly healed!

Don't accept sickness or disease! People will often tell me, "Well, you don't know what the doctor said!" That's true, I don't, but I do know what God's Word says, and it comes down to a choice. Whose report are you going to believe? What are you willing to accept? If you believe the Word of God, then you have to believe that God wants you well.

Smith Wigglesworth, the great British evangelist of the past, was asked to pray for a man who had come forward with severe stomach pain. Wigglesworth became outraged at the devil for inflicting this kind of suffering upon the man. Commanding the pain to be gone, he punched the man in the stomach so hard it knocked him off his feet. When the man was able to stand, he did so completely healed! This was not an isolated incident. Wigglesworth used this method several times during the course of his healing ministry.

Please hear me, I am not instructing you to punch sick people! What I am saying is that it's time we become angry at Satan and stop accepting what he tries to inflict on us!

Several years ago, while ministering in Argentina, we were privileged to visit with and observe, evangelist Carlos Annacondia during mass crusades. We couldn't help but notice how visibly upset he would become when he ministered and prayed. A local missionary explained that Carlos was mad at what the devil was doing in people's lives, and in his anger, he would literally scream at the devil for about twenty minutes, declaring him a defeated foe and demanding that he bow to the authority of Jesus!

We may not use the same method, but we need to be just as adamant in the declaration of our covenant right to healing. We should be just as upset as Carlos about what the devil has done—either in our bodies, or to the people we are ministering to.

Jesus paid the highest possible price for our spiritual, physical, and emotional wholeness. Suppose parents purchased wonderful gifts for their child, wrapped them carefully, put the child's name on the tags, and set them before the child. Can you imagine how hurt a parent would be if the child refused the gifts saying, "No thanks, I don't need that."

Jesus has already paid for your healing—you might as well take it. It brings Him joy when you take His gifts. If my health makes Him happy, then I choose health!

---

[1] John 10:10.
[2] John 5:6, ESV.
[3] John 5:7, NLT.
[4] John 5:8, NLT.

Chapter Seven

Tithes and Offerings

"Will a man rob God? Yet you have robbed Me! But you say, 'In what way have we robbed You?' In tithes and offerings. You are cursed with a curse, For you have robbed Me, even this whole nation. Bring all the tithes into the storehouse, that there may be food in My house, and try Me now in this," says the Lord of hosts, "If I will not open for you the windows of heaven and pour out for you such blessing that there will not be room enough to receive it" (Malachi 3:8–10).

A lot of people get highly offended when money is linked to the blessings of God, or with healing. It has been our experience, though, that those who get upset over this topic aren't givers. People that don't tithe or give offerings are most often the very ones who take issue with this. But the Bible is very clear on the matter. Withholding your tithes and offerings will block the blessing of God and block healing.

Malachi tells us that if you're not tithing, you're robbing God, and the windows of heaven will close. It is very difficult to see people healed if the windows of heaven are closed. But, he continues, when we do tithe, we open the windows of heaven—and when the windows are open, that's when the blessings flow!

You cannot buy your healing. I want to be very clear about that. Not only could you never afford the cost of your healing, but it has already been paid for! Jesus has paid for it on Calvary. Healing is a free gift, just like salvation, but we must fulfill the conditions God set out, including releasing finances to Him.

Some disregard the principle of tithing as an Old Testament practice. In fact, a man once said to me, "I don't believe in that tithing thing—it's Old Testament." I answered him by stating that we believe the whole Bible, Old and New Testaments, and that just because it's in the Old Testament does not mean that it's not true. Secondly I said to this gentleman, "Yes, we believe the Old Testament teaching that ten percent from any source belongs to God, but let's look at the New Testament church. The Book of Acts church, the first New Testament church, didn't tithe. They sold everything they had and gave all!" The man quickly decided to take another look at tithing.

Instances of tithing are seen throughout the Bible. In fact, before the law of tithing was given in Leviticus, Abraham was practicing the tithe in Genesis! It's a biblical principle that works—and it is not just an Old Testament concept. In Matthew, Mark, and Luke, one out of every six verses deals with money! Of the twenty-nine parables Christ told, sixteen deal with the issue of people and their money. Jesus himself endorsed tithing and even went so far as to tell the rich young ruler in Luke 11 to sell all he had and give it away!

J.D. Rockefeller once said, "I never would have been able to tithe the first million dollars I ever made, if I had not tithed my first salary, which was $1.50 per week."[1]

There has been an ongoing discussion on the definition of a tithe in today's society. The question often arises, "Should the tithe be based on gross or net income?" My answer simply is that we should never be afraid to give too much to God! Captain Levy, a believer from Philadelphia, was once asked how he could give so much to the Lord's work and still possess great wealth. The Captain replied, "Oh, as I shovel it out, He shovels it in, and the Lord has a bigger shovel."[2]

Consider this: every week a young man goes to the corner store and openly shoplifts. The storeowner, a kind and compassionate man, watches him steal week after week and says nothing. This continues for months, and even years, until something happens; the young man is faced with a financial crisis. He approaches the storeowner for some help, groceries, or cash—anything to get him past his current crisis. The storeowner naturally replies, "I've watched you steal from me week after week, and now you have the audacity to ask for my help?"

It would make sense if the storeowner didn't help the young man. I can understand that. I can also understand how God could choose not to bless me, if I were robbing Him. That's what believers do when they withhold their tithes. Robbing God closes the windows of heaven.

There are those who like to brag about the fact they tithe, much like the Pharisee in Luke 11. Honestly, tithing does not give you bragging rights. When we tithe, we stop robbing God. Malachi 3 clearly shows us that the tithe belongs to God. We cannot rob from God and expect Him to consistently heal us! As I've stated before, God heals unbelievers—He also heals people that don't tithe. But I'm not talking about getting healed once in a while. I'm talking about living consistently in the blessing of God. I'm talking about being able to minister consistently in the blessing of God. God wants to open the windows of heaven. He is waiting to pour out such a blessing that you won't be able to contain it—but you have to give God what's rightfully His.

Most Christians say they believe the Bible, but by their actions demonstrate that they don't. It's a sad fact, but one that is evident, especially in the area of tithes and offerings.

Clive Pick, a respected minister and author, teaches that if ten percent of a congregation tithes, the windows of heaven will open only ten percent of the way for that church. This goes a long way toward explaining why it is so hard to see people healed and saved! Think of how easy it would be to receive if ninety percent of the people in a church tithed! The windows of heaven would be open ninety percent. People would get healed walking in! It would be so easy!

Recently, Gwen and I ministered in a church that was alive with God's presence. The congregation entered in fully during worship and expressed their love for the Lord, their pastor, and for each other in many tangible ways. When I began to minister, I asked those who had received healing to come forward and stand in the altar area. Only a scattering of people was left in their seats! There were so many, it would have taken hours to interview all of them. I randomly selected people throughout the group. Each one related amazing accounts of their past condition and demonstrated the miracle they had received.

The next day the pastor was telling us how blessed he is to lead these wonderful, giving people and estimated that at least ninety percent of the congregation tithed! It was a confirmation of Clive Pick's belief that the proportion of blessing is directly linked to the proportion of people who tithe.

God is a good God, who wants to see His people prosper and be healthy! He is waiting, ready to heal, bless, and prosper you. The moment we stop robbing God, the windows of heaven open, and when they do, get ready for miracles!

---

1 W.A.Crisswell, *A Guidebook for Pastors* (Nashville: Broadman & Holman Pub., 1980) p. 50.

2 *Today in the Word,* July 1990 (Chicago: Moody Bible Institute, 1990) p. 28.

Chapter Eight

Conclusion

In recent years, the Lord has been speaking to me, telling me that we were to raise up an army of healing evangelists. Some will be in full-time ministry, but many will be in the workplace, neighbourhood and places of business. They will lay hands on their co-workers in the office, they'll minister in stores and in their homes—everywhere they go, they will lay hands on the sick, and the sick will recover.

Jesus commissioned every believer in the Book of Acts to have a healing ministry. It's a sad commentary when, today, there are very few people in the body with a healing ministry. We all need to pray for the sick and see them healed. God wants to use *you* in healing.

Perhaps you've laid hands on the sick and they haven't recovered. Perhaps you've been praying for a touch in your own body and haven't seen the breakthrough you need. Review the six keys to breakthrough, and let the Holy Spirit search your heart. Are any of these areas an issue?

1. *Unconfessed Sin*—Is there something in your life that is not pleasing to God?

2. *Honour*—Do you honour your parents? Do you honour your spouse?

3. *How do you speak about others?*—Do you gossip or speak negatively about other believers?

4. *Unforgiveness*—Are you holding onto a grudge? Is there someone who has wronged you, that you have not forgiven?

5. *Acceptance*—Have you accepted the condition? Have you befriended your ailment?

6. *Do you tithe?*—Or are you robbing God?

Once you go through these six keys and submit to the changes the Lord reveals to you, I think you'll be amazed at how easy it is to receive your breakthrough. Gwen has experienced it first-hand. It's as if a light comes on, and when you follow the steps—whether it's confession, honouring, guarding your tongue, forgiving, standing against sickness, or tithing—healing is released!

The Apostle Paul tells us we must be spiritually prepared. He says, *"Put on the whole armor of God...."*[1] He tells us we should be equipped with the belt of truth, breastplate of righteousness, shoes of peace, shield of faith, helmet of salvation, and the sword of the Spirit. All of these defensive and offensive weapons will prepare us for every onslaught of the devil. But I believe Paul was thinking of people like you and me, who might argue, "I've done it all, but I'm still waiting for the victory." That's why he added, *"and having done all, to stand."*[2]

That's the secret! Never give up! Don't allow the enemy to discourage you, if you don't see an immediate answer. Examine your heart, line your life up with God's conditions for breakthrough, pray the prayer of faith, stand on God's Word, and persist until you receive! Stand, and see the victory come!

---

[1] Ephesians 6:11.
[2] Ephesians 6:13.